Images of War
Fighting in Ukraine: A Photographer at War

David Mitchelhill-Green

Pen & Sword
MILITARY

First published in Great Britain in 2016 by
PEN & SWORD MILITARY
an imprint of
Pen & Sword Books Ltd,
47 Church Street,
Barnsley,
South Yorkshire.
S70 2AS

A CIP record for this book is available from the British Library.

ISBN 978 1 47384 866 5

Printed and bound by CPI UK

Pen & Sword Books Ltd incorporates the Imprints of
Pen & Sword Aviation, Pen & Sword Maritime,
Pen & Sword Military, Wharncliffe Local History, Pen & Sword Select,
Pen & Sword Military Classics and Leo Cooper.

For a complete list of Pen & Sword titles please contact
Pen & Sword Books Limited
47 Church Street, Barnsley, South Yorkshire, S70 2AS, England
E-mail: enquiries@pen-and-sword.co.uk
Website: www.pen-and-sword.co.uk

Contents

Acknowledgments

My sincere appreciation is extended to the following individuals and their collective expertise who helped make this book possible: Walter and Hildegard Grimm, Claus and Lydia Grimm, Bob Johnston, Ian Hulley, Holger Erdmann, Diedrich Schwenker, Andrij Makuch, Henning von Husen, Patrick Egan, Kerry Miller, Martin Goretzki, Dr Yuriy Kvach, Dr Petra Bopp, Greg Singh and Lesley Roebig. Many thanks also to the enthusiastic staff of Pen & Sword: Roni Wilkinson, Jodie Butterwood, Matt Jones and Barnaby Blacker.

Foreword

The outcome of the Second World War was decided on Germany's Eastern Front. Penning a letter home from Crimea in early May 1942, a German Landser (or foot soldier) complained of the 'hollow accounts' of the fighting composed by 'incompetents' in senior positions. Angered by these reports, which 'recounted so many details and in the process forgot the everyday life of the war, the actions of simple soldiers,' he described how the 'simple infantrymen' were, in his mind, the 'heroes'. Walter Grimm, a professional photographer conscripted into the German Army, captured the images in this book, a private chronicle of 'simple soldiers' training for war and serving in Ukraine during 1941-43. Grimm's record of the fighting in Ukraine is presented here in its entirety for the first time.

Introduction

Adolf Hitler's decision to invade the Soviet Union in June 1941 – the largest military clash in history—was a gamble. Despite Otto von Bismarck's earlier warning against invading Russia and the peril of fighting a war on two fronts, Germany's Führer boasted: 'We have only to kick in the door and the whole rotten edifice will come crashing down.' In private, however, Hitler was more cautious. Confiding his fears to Herman Göring, he explained that 'It will be our toughest struggle yet – by far the toughest. Why? Because for the first time we shall be fighting an ideological enemy, and an ideological enemy of fanatical resistance at that.'

In the months preceding the invasion, codenamed Operation Barbarossa, weapons, vehicles and personnel were moved across Europe, on an unparalleled scale, to an 820-mile front line stretching from Finland to Romania. The 3.2 million German troops were buttressed by a further 600,000 troops from Hitler's allies and puppet states, including 250,000 Romanians, 300,000 Finns and 50,000 Slovaks. (In time a division of Spanish volunteers, SS recruits from across Europe, and troops from Italy, Hungary and Croatia would join the 'European crusade against Bolshevism'). The massive German invasion force was equipped with 3,332 tanks, more than 7,000 artillery pieces, some 60,000 motor vehicles and 625,000 horses. Aside from a small number of elite motorized divisions, the majority of the infantry still marched on foot, as Napoleon's men had done in 1812; indeed the French emperor's legions had reached the gates of Moscow faster than General Heinz Guderian's panzers would.

Barbarossa was assigned to three army groups: *Generalfeldmarschall* Fedor von Bock's Army Group Centre was to destroy the Soviet forces in White Russia before driving northward to crush the Red Army based in the Baltic area. This was to be achieved in concert with a thrust from *Generalfeldmarschall* Wilhelm Ritter von Leeb's Army Group North, driving from East Prussia towards Leningrad. Simultaneously, *Generalfeldmarschall* Gerd von Rundstedt's Army Group South was charged with annihilating Red Army formations defending the Ukraine before they could withdraw across the Dnieper River. All effort would then focus on the capture of Moscow. It was anticipated that the Soviet Government would collapse and the entire campaign would be over before winter, eliminating the need for operations in the snow and cold.

Stalin famously did not believe that Germany would attack and chose to ignore the multitude of warnings, believing them to be a ruse. Economic aid to his erstwhile ally continued with one of the last Soviet goods trains crossing the border only hours prior to the attack at 3.15 am on Sunday, 22 June 1941. Surprise, both strategic and tactical, was complete. Resistance from the Red Army border guards was quickly overcome with the exception of the fortress at Brest-Litovsk. But as Hitler's Ostheer drove deeper in the Soviet Union, it soon found itself woefully unprepared to operate across the vast territory; 'The distances in Russia devour us,' Rundstedt wrote to his wife. Of the 850,000 miles of road, only some 40,000 miles were sealed, all-weather roads. Thick dust, driving in low gear for extended periods and inadequate air filters reduced engine efficiency and increased fuel consumption. Indeed, more vehicles were lost due to the dreadful Soviet road system than through combat during the opening phases of the operation.

Armoured and motorized divisions racing ahead to encircle Soviet divisions left behind the foot-weary infantry and horse-drawn transport. Columns of empty trucks returning from the front and parties of *Eisenbahntruppe* repairing and converting Soviet railway lines to the standard European gauge partially filled the unoccupied vacuum. Just weeks into the advance, Gottlob Bidermann, a *Landser* in the Eleventh Army noted: 'Our lines of supply became more strained with each day's advance…The depth of our penetration into the Soviet Union began to take its toll, and ammunition rationing served as the first indication of the shortages that we were to encounter with disastrous results in future battles.'

Hitler's 1933 decision to motorize his army had led to the deterioration of the German railway network with fewer locomotives and rolling stock available to support the operation. It also placed an enormous economic emphasis on rubber and oil: two essential raw materials Germany lacked. Because the domestic automobile industry was unable to meet the growing military and civilian need, a heterogeneous mix of civilian and captured foreign vehicles was requisitioned – a quartermaster's nightmare and stopgap measure that Grimm's photographs readily detail. Incredibly, the Wehrmacht operated some 2,000 different types of vehicle in the Soviet Union; Army Group Centre alone required more than a million spare parts. As Bidermann explained: 'our army appeared to consist of vehicles of every type and description from half of Europe, sometimes making it impossible to obtain even the most simple replacement parts. We found ourselves growing envious of the uncomplicated Russian supply system. Although their inventory of weapons and equipment might not have been as varied or as specialized as our own, what they did have was reliable and could be logistically supported almost anywhere.'

German horses also suffered enormously in the Soviet Union. Exhausted by the harsh climate and enormous distances, breeds used to the temperate conditions in central Europe were also denied their usual diet of oats. As a substitute, straw was stripped from peasants' homes. Although regulations prohibited the requisitioning of local *Panje* horses, thousands of these sturdy animals became an essential part of the Wehrmacht's overextended supply system.

Five weeks into a campaign that was expected to rapidly smash a 'vastly inferior enemy', the Wehrmacht found itself overwhelmed by the demands of the battlefield. Against the advice of his general staff, Hitler shifted the focus of the invasion from capturing Moscow to seizing the Ukrainian 'breadbasket' and the Caucasus oil wells. Outwardly successful, Hitler's intervention netted a staggering number of Soviet prisoners in Ukraine: 103,000 men near Uman (south of Kiev) in early August; 665,000 around Kiev by 26 September in what was the greatest encirclement in history; 100,000 at Melitopol and Berdiansk (near the sea of Azov) by 10 October; and a further 100,000 at Kerch (in the Crimea) by 16 November. Yet none of these battles were decisive. As General Franz Halder, Chief of the *Oberkommando des Heeres* (OKH, the Supreme High Command of the German Army) noted, the Red Army was enduring a string of gigantic defeats, yet these enormous losses were also sapping the Wehrmacht's finite strength.

Ironically, it was at the height of success that Germany began to lose the war in a bloody contest of attrition, which only intensified the further it pushed east. After only a month of fighting, General Heinz Guderian's 4th and 17th Panzer Divisions were operating at thirty-five and forty per cent strength respectively. Unlike the Soviet colossus, which could concentrate its much larger population and growing military might on a single front, German forces were also deployed across much of Europe, as well as in the small but expensive sideshow in North Africa. With each new advance and encirclement, more and more German troops became casualties while the length and depth of the *Ostfront* expanded, irretrievably reversing Germany's fortunes. As one Panzer commander remarked, the inexorable march held the potential for the invading army 'to be destroyed by winning'. By mid-September 1941, a total of 460,169 German soldiers and non-commissioned officers were listed as casualties with another 16,383 officers listed as lost; and these figures did not include the tens of thousands of troops reported as sick. Fatally, Hitler's home army was unable to send adequate numbers of replacement troops. Moreover, the *Ostheer* was now suffering from the physical and mental exhaustion of continual fighting, declining armoured support and shortages of fuel and ammunition.

Nevertheless, by November 1941 Hitler's southern thrust had captured most of Soviet Ukraine. The ensuing scale of destruction and suffering, more than in any other European country, was unparalleled. Approximately thirty per cent of the population, or 6.8 million Ukrainians, were killed or died of from the effects of disease or starvation during the Nazi occupation. To alleviate the Third Reich's severe manpower shortage, some 2.3 million Ukrainians were deported to Germany as slave labourers (*Ostarbeiter*, or 'eastern workers').

Although Nazi policy initially forbade any form of collaboration with 'inferior' Eastern peoples, out of sheer desperation many commanders recruited Ukrainians wishing to fight against Stalin to bolster their thinning ranks (these local auxiliaries were known as *Hiwis*, from the German term *Hilfswilliger*, meaning 'willing helpers'). But the opportunity to harness the Ukrainians' deep-seated hatred of the Soviet system was essentially squandered. The forced deportation of Ukrainian *Ostarbeiter* (eastern workers) to the Reich particularly incensed the local population and encouraged many to join the Soviet partisans or the Ukrainian Insurgent Army, which fought against both German and Soviet forces.

Stalin, in the meantime, had received two months' grace on the Moscow front, his position further improved by America's entry into the war in December 1941. Granted a reprieve, the wounded but determined Red Army continued to grow in strength while Hitler's continued to wane. Former German general Friedrich Wilhelm von Mellenthin explained after the war that the drive on the Soviet capital, temporarily abandoned in August in favour of conquering Ukraine, may well have been decisive had it continued as the primary *Schwerpunkt* (focal point) of the invasion. Capturing the seat of Stalin's power might well have paralysed the Soviet war effort. The Wehrmacht, however, had failed to rout the Red Army in a swift victory. Barbarossa had failed.

Fear of a protracted campaign extending through the winter began to haunt the invading army. As early as 3 August, General Gotthard Heinrici contemplated what lay ahead: 'We wonder sometimes what winter will bring. We will certainly have to remain here in Russia…So we will have to endure a positional war along an enormous front.'

The Soviet *rasputitsa* – the wet period in autumn and spring when rain and melting snow turned dusty roads into a quagmire, 'a sea of sticky, clinging mud' – was followed by a bitterly cold winter. The frozen ground prevented men from digging in; German radiators and crank-cases cracked; weapons froze solid. Frostbite casualties began to eclipse the number wounded in combat, and nearly all troops suffered from diarrhoea.

Following its first disastrous winter, the Wehrmacht resumed the offensive in the south in the summer of 1942. Pushing into the Caucasus and reaching the Volga, German forces suffered a crushing defeat at Stalingrad – the biggest single defeat in the history of the German Army. The tide of war had long since turned by the time of Hitler's 1943 summer offensive, little more than a glorified local assault, which faltered at Kursk after a matter of days. A slow retreat began, the Germans leaving a trail of destruction in their wake.

Pushing steadily west, Soviet troops, with partisan support, liberated one Ukrainian city after another. Kiev was retaken on 6 November 1943 with nearly all of Soviet Ukraine liberated after the battle of the Korsun–Cherkassy Pocket (25 January-17 February 1944). The Eastern Front all but disintegrated after the defeat of Army Group Centre five months later. The Wehrmacht was now a shadow of its former self and within a matter of weeks the Red Army had reached the point from where Barbarossa was launched three years earlier.

Situation Map dated 12 January 1942 showing the German advance in Ukraine. Maps on a scale of 1:100,000 issued prior to the invasion were criticized for being old and of poor quality. One officer complained of a map dating back to 1870 with only the road running from Smolensk to Moscow shown. Captured enemy maps proved impossible for most Germans to understand with one officer in a panzer division complaining that they were only fit for toilet paper. Further confusion arose from villages within a small area having the same name. Units, naturally, became lost, which led to missed objectives, excessive fuel use and unnecessary vehicle wear.

Chapter I
Preparing for War

Lying in prone position, this soldier learns how to fire the Mauser Karabiner 98 Kurz (or K98), the Wehrmacht's standard bolt action service rifle. Chambered for 7.92x57mm ammunition, a conversion kit was also available for training that allowed the rifle to fire small calibre rounds. Entering service in 1935, the gun remained in use until the end of the war.

The Mauser K98 was a reliable and straightforward weapon to operate. After opening the operating bolt, a five-round charging clip was inserted. The cartridges were pressed down into the internal magazine and the bolt closed, which ejected the clip. The rear sight of the *Gewehr* (rifle) was graduated from 100 to 2,000 metres although the effective range was up to 500 metres. No adjustment was available for wind. An earlier importance placed on the volume of rifle fire delivered over accuracy was reversed after the invasion of the Soviet Union when accurate individual shooting was specified.

Marksmanship results were relayed by field telephone and recorded. This soldier wears the early pattern *Feldmütze* (field cap) with national emblem and Reich cockade. The bitter experience of the first Soviet winter lead to the introduction of a new and more practical pattern cap in 1942 with side flaps that could be unbuttoned and worn over the ears.

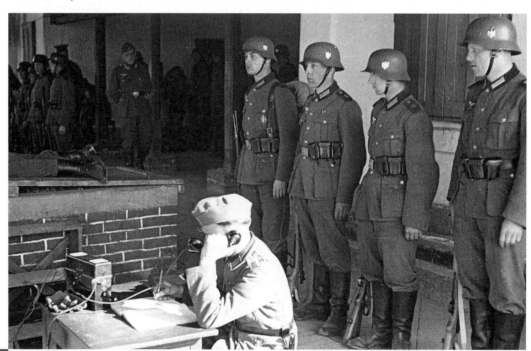

This *Landser* (foot soldier) wears the standard *feldgrau* (field grey) M36 tunic with dark green collar and shoulder straps. His trousers are tucked into the hobnailed *Marschstiefel* (marching boots). His belt holds a single ammunition pouch. Each compartment held ten clipped rounds. For head protection he wears a M1935 pattern *Stahlhelm* (helmet).

The K98 rifle was maintained using the cleaning kit M34 (*Reinigungsgerät* 34). An oiling or bore brush attached to a chain was pulled through the barrel for routine cleaning.

Rifles stacked, or piled, during a pause in training. Professor Friedrich Schwerd, designer of the iconic German *Stahlhelm*, recalled in a 1932 interview his idea for a one-piece steel helmet that could prevent 'the sort of shell fragment injuries which I had observed during surgical operations could surely be prevented'. The resulting M1916 helmet was authorized for wear in February 1916, the forerunner to the M1935 pattern *Stahlhelm*.

Basic training included strenuous day and night tactical exercises with live firing. In the realistic replication of combat, a one per cent fatality rate was considered acceptable. The basic training course for enlisted men in 1941 was at least three months.

Upon entering military service, all soldiers undertook a basic training course of six weeks before being assigned to permanent units. Note the telegraph wire in the background, indicating signals training.

Recruits receive instructions on wearing the *Gasmaske* 30 '*S-Maske*'. This rubberized canvas gas mask was manufactured in three sizes. Four different filters were issued: the Fe37, the Fe37 'R', the Fe41 and the Fe42. 'Fe' stood for '*Filter Einsatz*'; the number indicated the year it came into service.

Chapter 2
The Tyranny of Distance

Crossing the border from the *Generalgouvernement*, a German administrative region in Poland encompassing the borderlands of western Ukraine.

A motorized column passes Ukrainian refugees. The roadside sign carries a warning of disease risk and the associated hazard of drinking the water.

An assortment of clothing and equipment lying on a train station platform including: tunics, boots, M1934 pack with fur flap, mess kit, *Zeltbahn* (shelter quarter), belt with ammunition pouch, K98 rifles, *Gasmaskenbüchse* (gas mask canister) and bugle.

A Phänomen Granit 25, a type commonly employed as an ambulance, leads an Opel *Kapitän* staff car. Every German military vehicle carried a front and rear *Nummerschild* (number plate). The WH prefix indicated Wehrmacht *Heer* (ground forces).

A Fieseler Fi 156 *Storch* liaison aircraft flies above flatbed railway carriages being loaded with vehicles. Soviet rail construction standards were inferior to those of Western Europe with lighter rails usually laid on a bed of sand, instead of rock and gravel. The wider distance between rail sleepers also precluded the use of heavy locomotives.

Steam locomotives, vital to the Wehrmacht's enormous supply needs, faced numerous difficulties operating in the Soviet Union. Following the advice of a US railway engineer in the mid-1800s that an invader would have difficulty adapting to a different rail gauge, Czarist Russia (and subsequently the Soviet Union) adopted a wider rail gauge compared to the European standard. This safeguard forced the Germans to overhaul the Soviet network, and some with 21,000 kilometres of track re-laid by May 1942.

The harsh Soviet winter wreaked havoc on the Wehrmacht's rail supply system. Complex German locomotives were more susceptible to breaking down in the cold than the basic Soviet models. During the winter of 1941-42, seventy per cent of the German locomotives broke down; moreover only twenty per cent of the stripped-down German 'winterized' locomotives were operational at the end of 1941.

Manhandling an empty trailer onto a flatbed rail carriage. Prior to Barbarossa, the Soviets remodelled their western border rail centres for through traffic only. Marshalling yards and workshop facilities were moved east to prevent the Germans from using them in the event of an invasion—yet another unforeseen obstacle for the attacking army.

This steaming *Feldküche* (field kitchen) is a captured Russian type KP -3 -37(r): KP = *kuchnya polewaya* (Russian for field kitchen); 3=three boilers; 37=Year of introduction; r=Wehrmacht abbreviation for captured Russian equipment. Note the trailer's height, which presented problems when serving meals, and dual tyres.

A single axle trailer is brought forward for loading. Rail transport was the weakest link in the *Ostheer's* supply apparatus.

A French Matford V8-F917-F997WS truck is pushed into position on a flatbed carriage. Regulations stated that 'motor vehicles and tanks should be wedged in especially tight and lashed down with cables in order to prevent them from sliding.' Batteries were removed in cold weather and stored in heated passenger cars, and radiators were covered to prevent freezing in extreme cold.

The Mercedes-Benz Type 170 V was a common car in Wehrmacht service with 71,973 examples produced from 1935 to 1942.

The Citroen Type 45 U saw widespread use on the Eastern Front. Some 18,500 of these 73-hp French trucks were manufactured for the Wehrmacht from 1941 to 1944. Note the cold weather radiator cover.

The 3-ton Ford V8-51, successor to the Ford BB, was manufactured in Germany from 1937 to 1939.

The Ford Motor Company AG opened its Berlin plant in 1926. Nine years later it became an independent German automotive company, renamed Ford-Werke AG. By 1941 the company was under the direct control of the Nazi government with its headquarters in Cologne. Curiously, Adolf Hitler cited industrialist (and fellow anti-Semite) Henry Ford as his personal inspiration in a 1931 interview.

Rail transportation played a far more strategic role in the Soviet theatre than in earlier campaigns. Former *General der Infanterie*, Günther Blumentritt, recalled how the 'badness of the roads was the worst handicap, but next to that was the inadequacy of the railways, even when repaired. Our Intelligence was faulty on both scores, and had underestimated their effect. Moreover the restoration of railway traffic was delayed by the change of the gauge beyond the Russian frontier. The supply problem in the Russian campaign was a very serious one, complicated by local conditions.'

A bare-chested *Landser* poses for the camera in front of a Mercedes-Benz type L 1100. Note the standard issue military identification tag (*Erkennungsmarken*) around his neck. The German ID tag did not contain the soldier's name but the unit he was inducted into, a reference number and blood type.

Waiting to move out. The two *Landser* in the centre of the photograph are not wearing their identification tags. Wartime regulations specified: 'The soldier must wear his tag on a [80 cm] string around his neck; carrying it in his pack, his wallet, or a pants pocket is forbidden…' The *Sütterlin* script 'I' on the truck door represents an *instandsetzung*, or maintenance unit.

On watch for enemy aircraft. This open-topped *Deutsche Reichsbahn* anti-aircraft carriage is equipped with two tripod-mounted *Maschinengewehr* 34 or MG34 machine guns. The staff car behind the German shepherd dog in the first photo is a BMW 326 Cabriolet.

A close-up study of two gunners and their skyward-pointed MG34 machine guns. A superbly engineered weapon, fine tolerances nevertheless made it difficult to manufacture and rendered it susceptible to jamming by dust and sand. The MG34 was replaced by the MG42, a superior weapon both cheaper to produce and more reliable in combat conditions.

Chocking the wheels of a 1932 model Ford BB. Powered by a four-cylinder 52-hp engine, this truck was identical to the US manufactured version. The curved headlight support was straightened on the 1937 model.

Another former French truck is prepared for the rail journey east, this time a Delahaye type 103. Note the French rolling stock in the background with signage indicating capacity in men and horses. Operation Barbarossa would not have been possible without the wide scale use of foreign vehicles, although most were unsuited to Soviet conditions and promptly broke down.

A *Sonderkraftfahrzeug* (special purpose vehicle) Sd. Kfz. 6 half-track at a busy Ukraine railhead. In 1941 the Soviet Union consisted of 8,400,000 square miles of territory. Of the 52,000 miles of railroad track, less than fifteen per cent was classed as heavy capacity.

A huge miscellany of trucks and motorcycles were freighted east. In 1938 the Wehrmacht employed 100 different trucks, 53 types of car and 150 models of motorcycle. This excessive diversity prompted the 'Schell Programme', aimed at reducing the number of vehicles to thirty standardized types. But with passive resistance from the German auto industry and rising demand outstripping production of the new Schell vehicles, rationalization of the German motor pool in the Soviet Union proved impossible.

A round signal paddle is used to guide this FAUN (*Fahrzeugfabriken Ansbach und Nürnberg* AG) ZR wheeled tractor onto the carriage. Manufactured from 1938 to 1944 and powered by a 150-hp *Deutz* diesel engine, the ZRS model was modified to drive on rails.

Enjoying a meal in his *Kochgeschirr* 1931 (Mess Tin M31), this *Oberfeldwebel* (sergeant) sits beside a *Deutsches Reichspost* bag of mail for his men.

Feldpost (Field Post) mail is distributed during a break on the journey east. Letters, cards and small packets (up to one kilogram in the summer of 1941) could be sent to troops. Stamps were only needed for mail sent by air with each soldier receiving four *Luftfeldpost* (airmail) stamps a month.

Mitteilungen für die Truppe, a regular instructional leaflet published for non-commissioned officers (NCOs) praised letters from home as 'weapons', a 'type of vitamin for the spirit'.

Deutsches Rotes Kreuz (German Red Cross) nurses provide water to troops during a stop on the long journey east. A 1933 statute removed the organization's independence and made it an instrument of the Third Reich. Red Cross nurses formed part of the Wehrmacht's medical corps.

Vehicles belonging to Walter Grimm's telephone construction unit at the Stalino (today Donetsk) railhead in eastern Ukraine. Coal extracted from the Donbas region was found to be unsuitable for German locomotives while the water required an additive to prevent scaling in the boilers. Since Soviet locomotives were larger and carried more water than the German engines, the larger distance between water towers created an additional problem for the invading army.

Crossing the Dnieper

To cope with the ever-lengthening supply lines a huge variety of domestic and captured vehicles were requisitioned for service in the East. The following assortment of wheeled vehicles within a single unit was photographed crossing the Dnieper River on a *Bruckengerate* B pontoon bridge at Kiev (Kyiv).

Hansa-Lloyd *Dreitonner*. This model entered production in 1938, the same year the company name became Carl F.W. *Borgward Automobil- und Motorenwerke GmbH*.
In the background is St. Michael's golden-domed Monastery. The Germans captured the city of Kiev virtually intact although a Russian mine exploded in the former arsenal next to the monastery on 20 September 1941 killing German artillery officers and soldiers quartered there.

A 1937 pattern Ford BB truck. By the time of the Soviet invasion, the Wehrmacht was short some 2,700 trucks. Vehicle losses had outstripped production by August 1941. In November alone, 5,996 trucks were lost—double the actual production for the same month.

A French Matford V8-F917-F997W. Stalin was incensed that the French Army had failed to destroy its vehicle stocks before the 1940 armistice; the occupied territories (chiefly France) subsequently manufactured 39,574 trucks in 1941 and 37,163 in 1942 for the Wehrmacht.

Magirus, either a type M 25, M 27 or M 30. A total of 8,569 of these vehicles were produced from 1933. Taken over by Humboldt-Deutz AG in 1936, the Magirus marque was retained until 1939.

This vehicle is most likely a Krupp LD 4 M 232: L = *Lastwagen* (truck); D = diesel; 4 = 4-ton payload. Krupp profited from the war in the east by using European slave labour in its Essen armaments works while industrialist Alfred Krupp (who became head of the company in 1943) supervised the takeover of the Ukrainian iron and steel industry.

Mercedes-Benz trucks, either type L 1500 or L 2000. Note the stylized Soviet gas mask headlight covers.

Magirus L 235. Powered by 85-hp four-cylinder Deutz diesel engine, 2,070 of these trucks were manufactured from 1937 to 1940.

BMW 326 Cabriolet. Powered by a 50-hp, six-cylinder engine, this medium-sized civilian cabriolet, with its characteristic two-part bumper, was manufactured from 1936 to 1941.

Mercedes-Benz L 3000 S. Note the bomb emblem in place of the Gottlieb Daimler's iconic 3-pointed star. Approximately 16,000 examples of this 3-ton vehicle were produced from 1938 to 1944. It was not as popular with troops who preferred the more reliable Opel Blitz (Lightning) 3-ton series with its superior cross-country performance.

Servicing a Hanomag (*Hannoversche Maschinenbau* AG) SS 100 tractor. This military version of a 95-hp civilian road tractor, known as a *Gigant* (giant), was produced from 1936 to 1945. Production continued after the war with the vehicles known as the ST100 and ST100W, some of which served in the French Army.

Some 1,200 French V-8 Matford trucks were produced before the fall of France in June 1940. Manufacture resumed under the German occupation with the more powerful F 997 WS model replacing the F 917 WS model in 1941. The vehicles, however, were criticized by German troops for being unreliable and poorly built.

Dressed in a heavy sheepskin overcoat, a sentry stands beneath an elaborate sign displaying a *Feldpost* number, a unit's unique 5-digit postal address. Mail encoded with this system helped maintain secrecy regarding troop movements. *Feldpost* number 37484 belonged to the telephone networks construction unit: 3. *Fernsprech-Bau-Kompanie* 649 (3 Telephone Construction Company, Motorized 649).

Signposts underscored the tyranny of distance and the enormity of the Soviet Union. Gorlowka (also known as Horlivka) is a town located in the Donetsk Oblast (province) of eastern Ukraine.

Pumping fuel by hand from 200 litre drums into the ubiquitous, robust 20 litre fuel-carrier (*Wehrmacht-Einheitskanister*), which the Allies copied and nicknamed the 'Jerrycan'. The combination of poor Soviet roads, a paucity of good maps, and engines clogged with dust, greatly increased fuel consumption. Taxing an already overextended supply system, the Germans faced the challenge, in July 1941, of providing 12,000 tons of fuel daily.

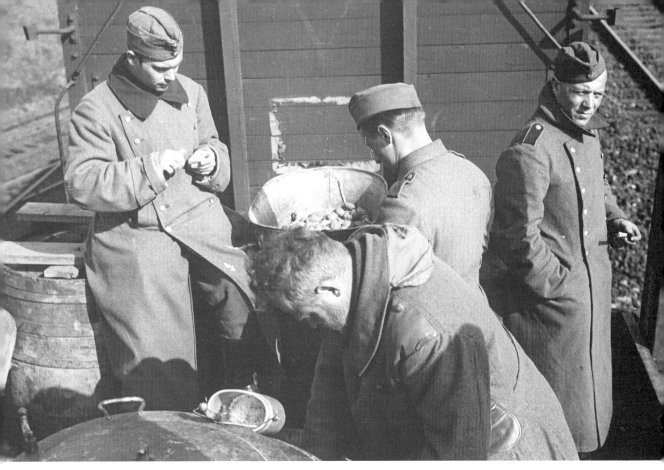

Peeling potatoes during a long railway journey east. The weather is cool with most men wearing greatcoats. The German soldier spent his first winter in the Soviet Union equipped with only his summer uniform, greatcoat and blanket.

Surely a welcome addition to the usual field rations. The *Landser* in the centre wears the SA Sport Badge, an award in three classes for excellence in defined physical, defence and field exercises.

Using the rear of a flatbed rail car as a makeshift latrine. The onset of the bitterly cold Russian winter, as one soldier noted, 'seemed to stop most of our natural functions'. There were 'many cases of cystitis and the inability to urinate quickly as well as the intense burning sensation which accompanied the act.' General Heinz Guderian noted that 'many men died while performing their natural functions.'

'Mobility', noted Napoleon, 'is the keynote of war.' The primitive Soviet road system placed enormous demands on vehicles' tyres. Germany's chronic rubber shortage was made even worse after the invasion of the Soviet Union by the severing of natural rubber supply routes from eastern Asia.

Kriegsberichter (war correspondent) Erich Peter Neumann wrote of the privations in Ukraine in a February 1942 article in the propaganda magazine *Signal*: 'You have to talk of the roads when you talk of this war. And when those who have covered these roads hesitate in the telling of their experiences, and become silent thinking over the events in that chapter of their life, you need only to look at their weather-beaten faces. Their eyes reflect their sufferings, and he who has eyes to see discovers that these sufferings were very great… Six hundred and fifty miles separate us from the frontier of Germany…'

Engine maintenance on a Mercedes-Benz L 1100 truck. These 1.1-ton vehicles were manufactured from 1932 to 1937. Emblazoned with the word 'diesel' on the radiator, Daimler-Benz at the time believed their compression-ignition engines were the benchmark of contemporary design and production.

Thousands of Red Army GAZ-AA trucks were captured and used on the Eastern Front. While easy to maintain, employing Soviet trucks further exacerbated the problem of standardization. Such was the desperate need for captured Soviet trucks that a firefight broke out between units of the German VIII Army Corps and requisition squads after the 1941 battle of Smolensk.

Fixing the broken leaf spring suspension of a Soviet GAZ-AA. These basic vehicles were simpler and generally more reliable than their complex Western European counterparts. German mechanics, however, faced the challenge of fixing numerous different models, especially as the war progressed and greater numbers of captured and requisitioned civilian vehicles were pressed into service.

A replacement engine is hoisted using a block and tackle in a makeshift field workshop. Forward overhaul, unlike the opening campaigns of the war, became a major problem during the protracted Soviet campaign. Workshops for major repairs during the opening months of the invasion remained to the rear in Poland and Germany.

Home was far away. As the push into the Soviet Union deepened, so the front widened and Germany's supply lines lengthened.

A Wander W45 staff car is ferried across one of the 23,000-odd rivers that crisscross Ukraine. Powered by a 2.3 litre 55-hp engine, this vehicle was a competitor to the Mercedes-Benz 170V.

Posing beside a Mercedes-Benz 170V (W136) Sedan. Powered by a 1.7 litre four-cylinder 38-hp engine, the base price of this car in wartime Germany was 3,750 Reichsmarks.

Straightening the distinctive 'W' hood ornament of a Wanderer W45. The civilian number plates indicate that the vehicle was formerly registered to a police department in Ludwigsburg, Württemberg in southwestern Germany.

A German motorcycle with the distinctive Steib sidecar Nr28. A BMW designer sent to the *Ostfront* reported: 'we sought out the field repair shops, which operated in the most primitive conditions, directly behind the front line. There the machines were examined and reports on the troops' experiences were taken. My opinion was correct. The machines went under the liquid mud, which flowed over the motors by the bucketful and was sucked into the low-lying air filter, ruining it – the mud got into the motor, and often the oilpans no longer held oil, but only sand.'

BMW R35 motorcycle in front of two Ford staff cars: on the left is a Ford V8-G78A; on the right is a Ford V8-G48 cabriolet with bodywork by Drauz.

A Lanz Eil-Bulldog type HR9 D2531. Easy to maintain with few moving parts, the tractor's single cylinder hot bulb 55-hp engine could run on a variety of different fuels. More than 2,400 examples of this model Bulldog were produced from 1937 to 1944.

A Magirus L 235

Unlike field repairs, major vehicles repairs in the early campaigns were undertaken in maintenance shops on home territory. According to an Operational Report from the 198th Infantry Division in October 1941: 'The workshop company was swamped with work. Replacement parts from home could hardly be obtained. Instead, broken-down vehicles had to be stripped and completely abandoned in hope of later repair.'

Numerous French Unic Kégresse P107 half-tracks served in the Wehrmacht after the fall of France. These somewhat unreliable vehicles were designated *Leichter Zugkraftwagen 37 Unic* (f) or Zgkw. U 304 (f). The forward-mounted roller was used to cross ditches and overcome obstacles.

The uneven Soviet roads punished the weaker suspension systems of civilian cars and trucks operated by the Wehrmacht. The lower ground clearance of these makeshift military vehicles led to frequently broken oil and transmission sumps. Captured stocks of low-octane Soviet petrol could only be used with a benzol additive.

The retreating Red Army blew up the centre spans of the arched bridge spanning the Dnieper River at Dnipropetrovsk in eastern Ukraine. Note the Soviet trenches in the foreground.

Overseeing the ferry operation. The leather chinstrap on his M41 uniform cap places this Deutsche Reichsbahn employee in the lowest rank and pay group.

Wheels on tracks on water. A vehicle transport train is ferried on a barge across the Dnieper River near Kherson, a southern Ukraine crossroad between Kiev in the north and Crimea to the south.

Chapter 3
Communications

Telegraph poles loaded onto a flatbed rail carriage from an *Anhänger* (1achs.) *für Fernsprechbau* (Sd. Ah. 21), a military trailer consisting of two identical single axle trailers coupled together. It had a carrying capacity of 3.7-tonnes.

The 3-ton *leichter Zugkraftwagen* Sd. Kfz. 11 light half-track vehicle was built from 1938 to 1945. A range of body types ranged from soft-skin to fully armoured. Regardless, these prime movers were costly and over-engineered for their primary role.

In 1941 the Germans introduced the *Drehkreuz* telephone line, a simple and efficient system that significantly reduced materials and manpower. The two individual wires could carry up to fifteen telephone channels simultaneously.

Erecting *Drehkreuz* lines across the vast and featureless Ukrainian landscape. Both the Army and the Luftwaffe erected roadside telephone lines. Army lines followed the left hand side of the road (in respect to the advance) and Luftwaffe lines the right.

Unreeling the bare wire strung on a *Drehkreuz* line. Partisans generally targeted the existing poorer quality and less important Russian telephone lines, with their numerous thick iron wires, over the simpler *Drehkreuz* lines.

Restoring a former Soviet telephone line on the southern Crimean coast. The background resembles a Red Army 'Dunkirk' following the withdrawal of Soviet troops by sea.

Drehkreuz telephone lines were generally erected fifty metres away from a road to prevent the poles being knocked down by vehicles. The inferior Soviet roads were usually wider than usual since drivers fought to dodge potholes and skirted churned-up areas. Note the trenches in the foreground.

Digging holes for telegraph poles using a tool known in German as a *Doppelspaten* (double spade) or *Lochspaten* (hole spade).

The *Feldfernsprecher* 33 (Field Telephone 33) was the standard field telephone during the war. The white panels on the Bakelite case contain the German phonetic alphabet on one side and information such as call signs on the other.

An *Obergefreiter* (corporal) behind the wheel of a two-door Hanomag tractor hauling a Sd. Ah. 21 trailer laden with telephone poles. Note the vehicle statistics on the door: the abbreviated Kfz number (vehicle ordnance nomenclature), *Leergewicht* (empty weight in metric tons), *Nutzlast* (payload) and *Verlade Klasse* (railway shipping loading class).

The *Drehkreuz* telephone system had the practical advantage of using thin, freshly cut trees in situations where regular telephone poles were unavailable.

Porcelain electrical insulators are prepared…

…before they are screwed into telephone poles to support the bare wire cables.

Horch in Zwickau and Ford Germany in Cologne manufactured the *schwerer geländegängiger Personenkraftwagen*, or *s.gl. Einheits-Pkw* (heavy cross-country passenger car) from 1937 to 1942. These purpose-built V-8 vehicles, using standardized components, were designed to replace the Wehrmacht's hodgepodge of civilian vehicles.

This *Mittlerer Zugkraftwagen* Sd. Kfz. 6 type BN9/9b medium half-track was built by Büssing-NAG. Note the *Kfz-Nachtmarschgerät* (night driving device) on the front left mudguard. Introduced in 1939, this helmet-shaped device directed light ahead of a vehicle at night that was not visible from the sky or to ground observers.

Erecting a *Drehkreuz* telephone line. In the background are a Wanderer 23 (on the left) and a Wanderer 240. Production of Wanderer civilian vehicles ceased in 1941 when production switched to licence-built military vehicles. Part of Auto Union, the Wanderer marque ended with the cessation of hostilities in May 1945.

A French Unic Kégresse P107 half-track crosses a field of sunflowers. The Germans discovered in their first Soviet winter that sunflower oil was a superior acid-free alternative to their own lubricants, which froze in sub-zero temperatures. Enormous volumes of sunflower seeds and oil were also shipped to Germany for domestic use.

Looking over the driver's shoulder aboard a Unic Kégresse P107 half-track, one of 3,276 such vehicles built for the French Army. Many captured examples were modified in Wehrmacht service including an armoured personnel carrier version.

The *mittlerer Zugkraftwagen* Sd. Kfz. 6 engineer version had a driver compartment, three rows of passenger seats, and no rear storage compartment.

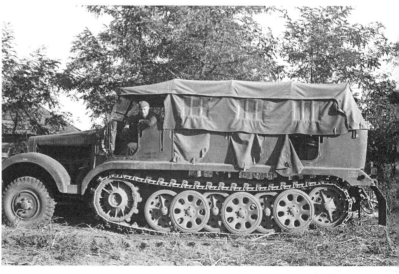

Unloading spools of bare telephone wire. The *Blankdrahtfreileitung* (uninsulated) bronze 3-mm *Felddauerleitung* (air-line) wire could convey signals without the need for amplification over a distance of 425 kilometres.

Jackknifed. A Sd.Ah. 21 trailer carrying telegraph poles and towed by a Kaelbler Z 4 G 110 tractor.

Rear view of a Sd. Ah. 21 trailer complete with dog kennel.

Erection of *Drehkreuz* lines in Crimea; the Black Sea is visible in the background. The men wear the dark green *Drillichrock* tunic.

According to former *General der Nachrichtentruppen* (Signal troops) Albert Praun: 'The new Drehkreuz lines proved amazingly sturdy…in spite of the tremendous strain which was placed on the personnel and their equipment [the signal communications system] did not suffer the same unexpected losses as did the railroad and motor vehicle traffic.'

Erecting telephone poles became even more difficult during winter once the ground froze. Repairing *Drehkreuz* lines damaged by wind, ice or shelling, however, required only one tenth of the time required for the older style telephone lines which had several wooden crosspieces carrying numerous lines.

General der Nachrichtentruppen (Signal troops) Albert Praun: 'In spite of the cold, the icy wind, and our inadequate winter equipment and clothing, the bare-wire lines were pushed farther and farther forward…there was still always enough work to do in constructing and maintaining new lines. On these occasions work up on the poles was not very pleasant…'

Chapter 4
Crimea

Crimea was technically part of the Russian Soviet Federated Socialist Republic at the time of the German invasion, having been given autonomous republic status within Russia after the Bolshevik revolution. Under German occupation, Crimea formed part of the *Reichskommissariat Ukraine*. In 1945 it became the Crimean Oblast, an administrative region of Russia, until 1954 when the then Soviet leader, Nikita Khrushchev, transferred Crimea to Ukraine. This was viewed as a 'gift' for Ukraine, whose population had suffered so terribly under the Nazi occupation.

German situation map of Crimea, dated 14 September 1942.

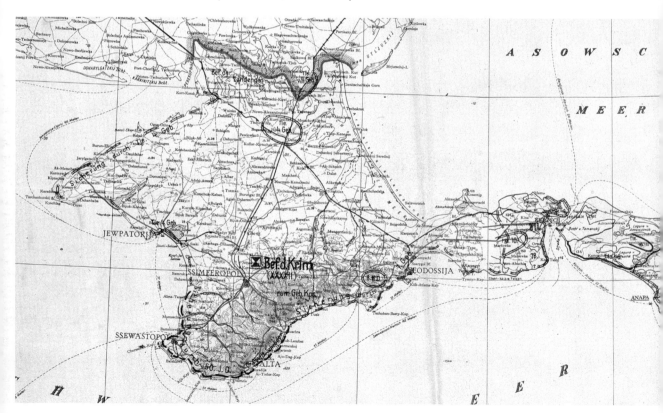

Pausing beside a French-built Delahaye 103 A truck on the dusty Bakhchisarai-Yalta road, outside Bakhchisarai in central Crimea. Production of this elderly model began in the late 1920s.

The *Marinefährprahm* (naval ferry barge) was a landing craft developed for the aborted 1940 invasion of England: Operation *Seelöwe* (Sea Lion). A total of 720 of these craft were built. MFP 306 was commissioned at Gollnow Shipyard, Stettin, on 19 June 1941. Assigned to the 3 *Landungsflottille* (3rd Landing Flotilla), this lighter was sunk by a bomb hit on the engine room at Kamysch-Burun, south of Kerch, on 30 November 1943.

Laid up at Yalta. *Marinefährprahm* F 144 was commissioned at the Varna shipyard, Bulgaria, on 25 March 1942. Assigned to the 1 Landungsflottille (1st Landing Flotilla), F 144 was badly damaged by two bomb hits (one of which was a dud) on the morning of 7 July 1943. The craft was subsequently salvaged and scrapped in October 1943.

A *Marinefährprahm* and *Pionierfähre* (Pioneer Ferry) are loaded in the bombed-out Kerch waterfront.

Pionierfähre (Pioneer Ferry) *PILF 219 ESSEN*, used by Construction Battalion 86, was sunk by a mine in the Kerch Strait off Taman on the east coast on 6 March 1943.

Four makes of truck including a Renault AGR, plus a Peugeot 202 car, parked outside the Simferopol *Soldatenheim* (literally, soldier's home), a club for off-duty servicemen.

Deutsches Rotes Kreuz nurses and soldiers outside the Simferopol *Soldatenheim*. Note the nurses wearing men's *Marschstiefel* in place of regulation lace-up shoes. According to a German handbook on winter warfare, such convalescent centres were 'successful without exception' in meeting 'an urgent need of troops'.

Pictured on the Yalta embankment. The Crimean resort town is best known for the conference on 4-11 February 1945 when US President Franklin D. Roosevelt, British Prime Minister Winston Churchill and Soviet Premier Joseph Stalin met to determine the future course of the war and postwar governance of Germany and Eastern Europe.

Driving through the Crimean mountains in a Horch 108 Type 40. The weapon at the ready is a captured Soviet Tokarev SVT-40 with early pattern 12-slot muzzle brake. Being short of self-loading rifles, the Germans used captured SVTs (*Samozaryadnaya Vintovka Tokareva* – Tokarev self-loading rifles) with the designation G.259(r).

The battered Sevastopol waterfront. After a costly 250-day siege, the Crimean port city and home to the Soviet Black Sea fleet fell to German and Romanian troops on 4 July 1942. The Red Army suffered 23,000 casualties and 95,000 men taken prisoner. Axis casualties numbered 35,866. Soviet troops later besieged and retook the naval fortress in May 1944 when remnants of the German Seventeenth Army sought refuge there.

The 185-ton Kriegsmarine *motortug* KEHL, pictured at Sevastopol, was built in 1930. Transferred from the Rhine to the Danube in 1941, she was transferred to *Seetransportchef Schwarzes Meer* (Maritime Chief Black Sea) in September 1943. Scuttled a year later at Prahovo, on the Danube, the tug was subsequently repaired and recommissioned.

A *Feldgendarme* (Military Policeman) checks a Luftwaffe Borgward B 1000 on the road to Sevastopol. Tasked with occupation duties, such as traffic control, by 1943 the *Feldgendarmerie* were also responsible for maintaining discipline within the ranks of the retreating Wehrmacht. Note the distinctive *Feldgendarmerie* gorget.

Approximately 5.7 million Red Army soldiers were taken prisoner. Of this number, it is estimated that between 2.5 and 3.3 million died in captivity: 845,000 in German camps near the front lines, 1.2 million in civilian-run camps in the rear, 500,000 in the *Generalgouvernement* of Poland and somewhere between 360,000 and 400,000 in camps within the Third Reich.

A specialist officer with the rank of *Sonderführer* addresses a crowd of Kuban Cossacks. *Sonderführer* were non-commissioned officers with a specific civil skill such as interpreting or engineering. They wore a standard military uniform, the primary difference between Army uniforms and those worn by a *Sonderführer* being the rank insignia.

Curiously, Nazi Germany did not classify Cossacks as *Untermensch* (subhuman), a derogatory label for Slavs, Roma and Jews. Serving in uniform for the Wehrmacht, Cossacks—a centuries-old military caste chiefly of Ukrainians and Russians—saw front-line service as 'co-combatants with equal rights' as well as in anti-partisan operations.

Having crossed the Kerch Strait to the western Caucasus, this *Landser* poses in front of Mount Elbrus, the highest peak in Europe and just visible in the background. A detachment of *Gebirgsjäger* (Mountain troops) reached the summit (5,642 metres) on 21 August 1942 and planted the swastika. The propganada coup, however, infuriated Hitler, who viewed the feat as grandstanding when his troops were needed for the drive south to Sukhumi in western Georgia.

Chapter 5
Occupation

Signwriting. 'Feldkommandantur' –
administrative sub-area headquarters –
normally commanded by an *Oberst* or
Generalmajor.

The Germans were initially welcomed as liberators in Ukraine with gifts of food and flowers. According to one Ukrainian, 'Many women were holding bouquets of flowers, which they threw at the soldiers and officers passing by. It was a rare case in history when the defeated rejoiced about the arrival of the victors.' The motorcycle is an NSU 601 OSL.

Kradmelder (motorcycle riders) served in a variety of roles such as scouts, couriers, spare parts carriers, even carriers of mail and hot meals. This motorcycle is a BMW R12 with sidecar.

Troops pose with their Wanderer cabriolet outside a Ukrainian *izba*. Propagandist Erich Neumann described these simple abodes for his western European audience: 'They consist of wretched peasant dwellings made of clay, but the same soldiers who until the beginning of the winter had entered them only with feelings of disgust, now defend these clay hovels like a costly possession. It is no longer important whether they consist of only one room, and it does not matter if every corner is full of vermin, the stove and the roof are all-important…'

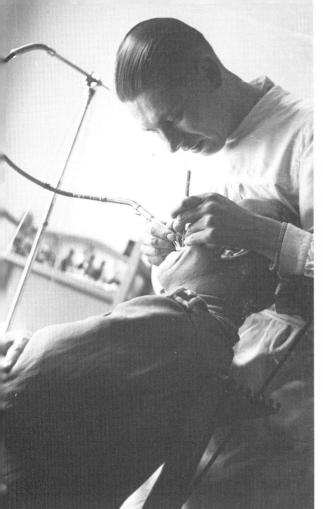

A field dentist in action. Each field hospital had a dental officer and specially trained assistant.

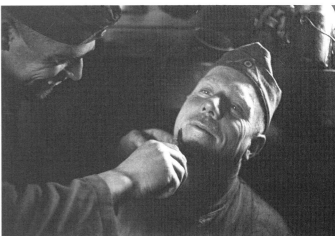

Although facial hair, apart from a trimmed moustache, was against regulations, rules regarding beards were often relaxed in the field, with beards common among *Gebirgsjäger* (mountain troops). Shaving in the morning was prohibited in severe cold weather.

German propaganda poster proclaiming 'Hitler the Liberator'. This popular portrait was initially displayed in many Ukrainian homes beside the religious icon. Later it appeared only to convey an appearance of loyalty as the brutality of the occupation became apparent.

Horse drawn troops of the Royal Hungarian *Honvéd* (Army). Drawn into an alliance with Germany on the pretext of regaining pre-First World War territory, Hungary declared war on the Soviet Union on 27 June 1941. Seven occupying divisions assumed control over large tracts of Ukraine, freeing up German security units. Hungary, however, paid dearly for its alliance with Germany with between 120,000 and 155,000 troops killed on the Eastern Front.

Local volunteers were known as *Hiwis*, an abbreviation of *Hilfswilliger* meaning 'willing to help'. As German losses mounted, so the need for extra manpower grew. Over time *Hiwis* accounted for up to forty per cent of some support units. The history of the 198th Infantry Division noted that the 'shaggy ex-Red Army men, who had fought bitterly against us just a short time ago, generally proved to be capable helpers. As long as they were treated decently, they behaved reliably, with scarcely any exceptions, and gained our respect and recognition.'

Approximately 2.3 million Ukrainians were deported to Germany as labourers. Many of these *Ostarbeiter* (eastern workers) willingly volunteered at the beginning of the occupation hoping to escape famine and unemployment and learn a new trade. After news of their poor treatment reached Ukraine, the Germans began using force to meet their quotas with towns and villages forced to register eligible workers. A failure by individuals to report led to the torching of homes and villages or detention in concentration camps.

A *Gefreiter* draws water from a countryside well. Stalin addressed the Soviet populace in a radio broadcast on 3 July 1941, calling for a scorched-earth policy to 'destroy all that cannot be evacuated' including railroads, food and water supplies. At the same time the Wehrmacht was marching forward in the expectation of largely living off the land.

These Sd. Kfz. 6 half-tracks show the evolution of paint schemes, from the early *Dunkelgrau* (dark grey) to the later *Dunkelgelb* (dark yellow), introduced in October 1942. As well as blending camouflage colours, a water-based white paint was also used during the winter snowfall.

Ukrainian peasants polish soldiers' black leather *Marschstiefel* at a railhead. Symbolic of the German infantryman, the hobnailed boots were called jackboots after the taller 'jacked' cavalry riding boots.

Enjoying a cup of coffee from a street vendor.

A horse and cart delivers *Essenbehälters* (food containers) with hot meals. The Wehrmacht relied heavily on horse-drawn transport with some three million horses and mules employed during the war. *Essenholer* (ration bearers) in fighting units would carry the heavy containers on their backs, often over long distances while exposed to fire.

Pork is on the menu. On 27 June 1941 Stalin decreed that 'All valuable materials, energy and agricultural materials, and standing grain' unable to be transported were to be 'destroyed, annihilated, and burned'. In practice the destruction of livestock mostly occurred in villages near main roads and many Ukrainian peasants hid their pigs from collective farm heads or *Komsomol* (young communist) members.

Field butchers prepare a pig for eating. Beef or pork, or a combination of the two, were the most common meats found in the German Army *Eintopf* (stew). Foraged meat, such as mutton, veal, or wild game was also used though German Army manuals warned that locally procured animals were to be examined by a veterinary officer before consumption.

Lunch is served from a small
'*Gulaschkanone*', in this instance a Hf.
14 *Feldküche* with wheels 'borrowed'
from a Soviet 45-mm AT gun type 37
or its limber.

The 'Kuchenbulle' (Kitchen Bull) was a slang term for a cook. Together with his assistants, a cook could feed between 60 and 225 men, depending upon the size of the *Gulaschkanone*.

While much of the *Ostheer's* food came from Germany and occupied countries, large amounts were also requisitioned or captured locally. The field cookbook *Östliche Speisen nach deutscher Art* (Eastern Dishes in German Style) published by Alfred H. Linde Verlag was specially produced for soldiers in the east.

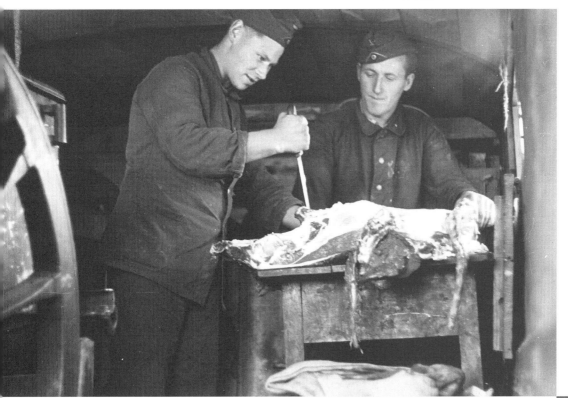

Lunch (*Mittagessen*) is served. Breakfast (*Frühstück*) was a cold meal such as coffee and bread. A hot lunch, such as *Eintopf* (stew), was generally the main meal of the day. The evening meal (*Abendessen* or *Abendbrot*) was mostly small.

A break from erecting and maintaining telephone poles provided the opportunity for a game of football. The 9 August 1942 grudge match between the Ukrainian FC 'Start' team and a German team at the Dynamo stadium at Kiev has become the stuff of legend—the so-called 'Death Match'.

Under review. *Stillgestanden*! (Attention!) An *Oberst-Leutnant* alights from his Horch vehicle to inspect a line of infantrymen. The colour piping on his cap would appear to be Artillery or a rear echelon service.

German and Cossack cavalrymen. Despite Hitler's July 1941 declaration that 'Only the German may bear arms, not the Slav, not the Czech, not the Cossack nor the Ukrainian,' a number of independent Cossack cavalry squadrons were formed under the First Panzer Army. Under their German commanders, long-range reconnaissance raids were undertaken.

German soldiers pose with requisitioned *Panje* horses. In a letter to his family dated 23 June 1941, General Gotthard Heinrici wrote how 'everywhere, our men take horses away from the farmers for our carriages, which causes wailing and howling in the villages. That's how the population is "liberated". But we need the horses…' As the 98th Infantry Division recorded, 'Without the little, unprepossessing Panje horses and their wagons and sleighs, our whole supply system would have come to a stop in the winter of 1941-42.'

Italian *Bersaglieri* (riflemen), recognizable by their distinctive feathered helmets, participated in the conquest of eastern Ukraine. According to Léon Degrelle, leader of the Walloon SS legion, 'One saw them everywhere, from the Dnieper to the Donets, small, swarthy, funny-looking in their two-pointed forage caps, or looking like birds of paradise under their *Bersaglieri* helmets from which projected, amidst the gusts of the steppe, a stately crop of rooster and pheasant feathers.' 'They detested the Germans,' noted Degrelle, who 'couldn't abide the Italians.'

A *Sanitätsgefreiter* (Lance Corporal in the medical corps) shares a cigarette with a comrade. The M42 tunic he wears lacks the pocket pleats of earlier pattern tunics, a measure designed to save material and time.

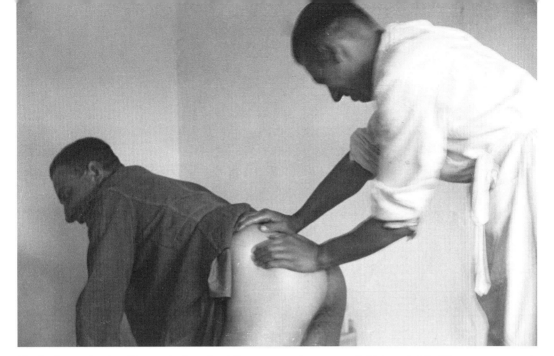

Medical examination. The majority of soldiers presenting at one field hospital in Kiev were treated for skin and sexually transmitted diseases. Having inspected the facility, an SS doctor observed that the 'emphasis no longer lay on clinical and surgical procedure.'

Buoyant *Gefreiter* (Lance Corporal) and *Obersoldat* (Private First Class) pose in front of captured French rolling stock. 'Stop!' reads the broken warning sign in Ukrainian; the other sign denotes 'The place to cross the track'.

Ukrainian peasants, mostly women, put to work as forced labourers on road construction.

Building a road across the seemingly endless Ukrainian landscape.

Informal group portrait before a Citroen Type 45 U truck. The other vehicle is an Opel Blitz. General Motors (GM) was an important manufacturer and source of latest technology for the Third Reich through its subsidiary *Adam Opel AG*. The parent company was encouraged to open a new plant in Brandenburg in 1935 to build the Opel Blitz exclusively for the Wehrmacht. Albert Speer, Hitler's former minister for armaments, admitted after the war that Germany could never have invaded Poland without access to GM's synthetic fuel technology.

Ford V8-G48 Cabriolet circa 1935-36, complete with trailer and puppy.

Machine-shop trucks contained equipment such as lathes, drilling machines and welding equipment. The vehicle on the right appears to be a Renault type AHN or AHR; the other vehicle is a field modification.

Oxyacetylene equipment is wheeled on a makeshift single axle trailer. The car in the foreground is a BMW 326; the truck in the rear is an Opel Blitz 2, 0-12 1-ton truck. After General Motors acquired Opel in 1931, many components were practically identical to Chevrolet light duty trucks manufactured in North America.

Some 37,000 blacksmiths served in the Wehrmacht. They regularly fabricated simple vehicle parts, otherwise unavailable, using a forge. Blacksmiths fell under the command of the divisional veterinarian.

Amused peasants observe the antics of these shirtless soldiers washing their garments. Note the tent in the foreground comprised of their individual *Zeltbahn* (shelter quarters) buttoned together to form a tent.

Posing in front of an *izba*, this *Landser* wears an early pattern tunic and *Feldmütze*.

The young greatcoated *Landser* beside the half-track wears the *Einheitsfeldmütze* M-43, a popular replacement field cap with flaps that could be lowered and buttoned at the front. Developed from a pre-First World War Austrian design, it remained standard headgear until the end of the war.

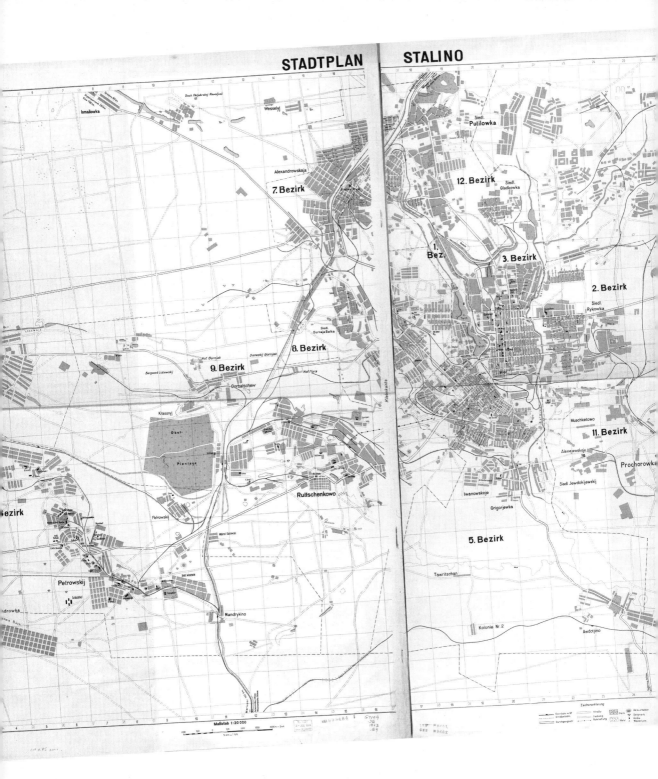

German map of Stalino, the largest city in the Donetz Coal Basin, dated 1943.

Stalino, what the Germans called the 'pearl of the Soviet Ruhr', fell to troops of the German XXXXIX Mountain Corps and Italian *Corpo di Spedizione Italiano* in Russia, or CSIR, on 20 October 1941. The massive steelworks, set up by the Welsh businessman John Hughes in1872, became the administrative centre of the Soviet Union's largest European mining district. Originally named Yuzovka, the city was renamed Stalino in 1924 and Donetsk in 1961.

These Soviet ideological statues were photographed at Park Shcherbakov, which opened in 1932 as a meeting place for Stalino steel workers.

The building housing the German *Soldatenkino* (soldier's cinema) survives to this day, as the oldest theatre in the city, as does the House of Soviets, built in 1929. Briefly reoccupied by the Red Army in March 1942, the Germans evacuated Stalino in early September 1943. According to a communiqué from Berlin, 'We evacuated Stalino according to plan in order to shorten the front, after the destruction of all military installations.'

Achsen Strasse ('Axis Street') ran through Stalino, named after Hitler's nemesis Generalissimo Joseph Stalin. The car in the foreground is a Horch 830 BL cabriolet.

German *Ski-Jäger* photographed at Stalino. 'There are no special "winter tactics",' a 1942 German handbook on winter warfare detailed. 'The hampering effect of deep snow, however, greatly influences the combat methods of normally organized and equipped troops. Ski troops and troops equipped with light sleds take over the missions assigned in temperate seasons to mobile troops (motorized, mounted and bicycle troops).'

Chapter 6
Dust, Mud, Snow and Ice

A supply column passes several captured Red Army *STZ-3* tractors. Manufactured at the Stalingrad Tractor Zavod (STZ), the vehicle's large air filter and wide tracks made it an ideal workhorse for local conditions.

The immense open spaces and monotonous landscape of the Soviet interior, so unlike Western Europe, proved psychologically challenging for the Germans. One soldier wrote of 'feeling eerily insecure', while another despaired, 'Nothing could have prepared us for the mental depression brought on by the realisation of the utter physical vastness of Russia. Tiny little doubts began to creep into our minds. Was it even possible that such vast emptiness could be conquered by foot soldiers?'

Marching through Ukraine, one soldier recorded how 'almost [throughout] the entire trek we were under dust like a gigantic grey cloud…dense, steep mountainous peaks [of dust].' Wrote another, 'The men marched in silence, coated with dust, with dry throats and lips.'

A dusty Opel 2.0 Litre sedan. A vehicle's interior, according to one soldier, offered no respite from the all-pervasive dust: 'in the column we now travelled as in a sandstorm. Clouds of dust penetrated through all the gaps in the windows… The wheels churned up fountains of sand that blacked out the sun.'

In his February 1942 *Signal* article, *Kriegsberichter* Erich Neumann waxed lyrical on German drivers: 'Not all these men have looked into the white of the enemy's eye, but every one of them, riflemen and gunners, anti-tank gunners and sappers, wireless signallers and riders, but above all the drivers of the wagons and lorries have fought against the country's neglected roads as though they were dangerous enemy weapons...'

Engine maintenance on a heavily camouflaged Sd. Kfz. 6 half-track. The tactical symbol behind the *Nachtmarschgerät* signifies the vehicle belonging to a *Fernsprechkompanie* (Motorized Telephone Company).

Cleaning the carburetor from an early model Opel Blitz with the air cleaner off to the side. An Operational Report from the 198th Infantry Division recorded that the 'motor vehicles had inconceivable engine troubles, for the fine sand got into everything and damaged pistons and cylinders. In addition they were so much too low-slung for this terrain, their chassis often hit bottom…'

Seemingly endless dusty roads stretched across Ukraine. Long before the invasion of the Soviet Union, Joseph Goebbels, Reich Minister of Propaganda, expressed a fear that 'I am refraining from publishing big maps of Russia. The huge size of the areas involved can only frighten our people.'

A captured Russian field kitchen model 1936 is towed past Ukrainian women washing clothing.

As early as July 1941 one soldier foresaw the difficulties that lay ahead: 'When I see even at this time of year how our vehicles, after it's rained a little, can barely make the grade, I just can't imagine how it will be in autumn when the rainy period really sets in.'

Resembling Napoleon's *Grande Armée*, the Wehrmacht brought together more than 600,000 horses from across Europe for the bulk of its transport needs in the Soviet Union. Interviewed after the war, former Field Marshal Gerd von Rundstedt attributed Germany's failure to crush the Soviet Union in 1941 in part to logistical difficulties: '…long before winter came the chances [of victory] had been diminished owing to the repeated delays in the advance that were caused by bad roads, and mud. The "black earth" of the Ukraine could be turned to mud after ten minutes' rain—stopping all movement until it dried. That was a heavy handicap in a race with time. It was increased by the lack of railways in Russia—for bringing up supplies to our advancing troops.'

Tremendous demands were made on men and horses. General Gotthard Heinrici, commander of the XXXXIII Army Corps, confided his unease to his wife in a letter dated 20 July 1941: 'The war here is without doubt very bad and to this must be added the tremendous road difficulties, the enormous spaces, the unending forests, the difficulties with the language and so on. All past campaigns seem like child's play in comparison with the present war. Our losses are heavy…'

Reduced to a standstill. According to former *General der Infanterie* Günther Blumentritt, 'Nearly all this transport consisted of wheeled vehicles, which could not move off the roads, nor move on it if the sand turned to mud. An hour or two's rain reduced the panzer forces to stagnation. It was an extraordinary sight, with groups of tanks and transport strung out over a hundred-mile stretch, all stuck…'

'The mud is now knee high,' a German soldier protested in October 1941. 'Many vehicles get stuck after the first few metres and can only be freed with the combined assistance of everyone present. Our drivers have now had experience in four campaigns… but the worst of the lot is undoubtedly the Soviet Union.'

A Soviet T-20 *Komsomolets* light artillery tractor under new ownership. Germany, Romania and Finland all used captured T-20s with some German examples armed with a 3.7-cm Pak 35/36 anti-tank gun. This vehicle is shown towing a former French Renault UK trailer taken from a Renault UE tankette.

The 'maddening mud', one German soldier wrote, was 'inconceivable' to those who had not experienced it first-hand. The spring *rasputitsa* was often worse than in autumn since the melting snow was accompanied by spring rains; 'terrible weather on the Eastern Front, wavering between freezing and thawing, heavy snow and rain, turned Ukraine into a glutinous sea of mud.'

A Sd. Kfz. 6 half-track, with improvised engine insulation to prevent the radiator freezing, tows an engineless truck outside a billeted *izba* (traditional dwelling). Writing in *Signal,* Erich Neumann observed that 'No soldier any longer speaks of what it was like in the dry dust of summer swarming with myriads of insects or in the grim and boundless mud of autumn, for the snow lying yards deep, beneath which the remains of the victims of that time sleep, the skeletons of the dead horses and the scrap metal of wrecked lorries provides sufficient new cares for topics of conversation in the evenings in the Soviet billets.'

A signals repair team and their horse-drawn sleds. 'The [icy] ground was so slick,' one soldier recorded, 'that the horses had difficulty even standing up.' The tough Russian *Panje* horses were superior to the German's best horses when vehicles were immobilized or unable to traverse muddy or snowbound roads. In early 1942 some Panzer Divisions—nicknamed '*Panje* Divisions'— were dependent upon several thousand of these horses since the majority of their vehicles were unserviceable.

A Bactrian camel in the service of the Wehrmacht. According to Russian war correspondent Vasily Grossman, Red Army soldiers found the 'tall and imposing animal visible at a great distance', which assisted their return to camp in appalling weather.

A report from the 198th Infantry Division in November 1941 recorded: 'What with the exertion, cold and lack of fodder, the condition of the horses worsened from day to day, and with it the division's mobility decreased more and more… Of an intended complement of 4,600, only 3,100 army horses are still alive, and fully 1,200 of them could scarcely stand up and were completely out of the question as draft horses… For the time being, 1,600 *Panje* horses had to take over…' The Germans lost 1,500,000 horses in the Soviet Union, mostly to injury, overexertion, malnutrition and freezing temperatures.

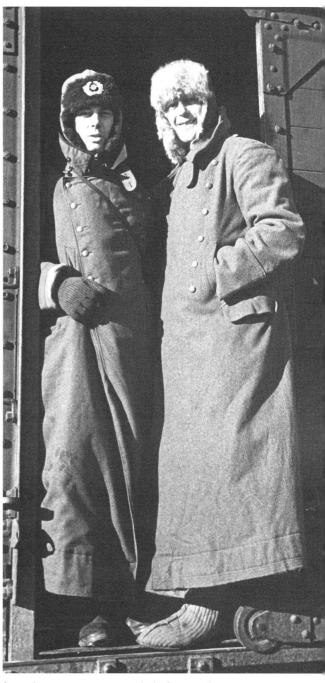

Flimsy straw overboots were hurriedly issued to soldiers forced to use appropriated clothing such as these *ushanka* fur hats. Wearers of these hats, despite the addition of Wehrmacht insignia, were sometimes fired upon by friendly troops. Of the cold, one soldier wrote: 'The cold numbed and deadened the human body from the feet up until the whole body was an aching mass of misery. To keep warm we had to wear every piece of clothing we owned.'

German freight cars, used as troop transport, were usually equipped with stoves, though for comfort troops were advised to cover the floor with straw and seal non-airtight walls with paper and straw. 'Misappropriation of stoves upon detraining' was forbidden.

Snow fences such as an *Ablagerungszaun* ('accumulation fence') proved effective in preventing snowdrifts on roads. It was recommended that snow fences were erected before the onset of winter and set up on both sides of the road, fifty to seventy feet from the shoulders. Small-grained sand, gravel or crushed rock was also sprinkled onto icy surfaces for traction.

Vehicles were started and run regularly in the cold to ease the strain on metal rendered brittle by sub-zero temperatures. A shortage of antifreeze led to some engines seizing while running. Oil resembled tar, fuel sometimes froze, and battery plates buckled. But, as ex-*General der Nachrichtentruppen* Albert Praun affirmed, 'In contrast to the infantrymen, who lacked winter clothing and of whom many froze just like their predecessors in 1812, the signal troops had the advantage that they could protect themselves better in their vehicles and carry clothes along with them.'

Roughly 1,600 trucks were required to equal the capacity of a double track railway line. Hitler's decision to motorize the Wehrmacht, however, led to fewer available locomotives and rolling stock plus an automobile industry incapable of meeting Germany's civilian and military needs.

Chapter 7
Detritus of War

Refugees pass an abandoned Soviet late production BT-7 (*Bystrochodnij Tankov,* or 'Fast Tank' type 7) tank. Armed with a 45-mm L/46 gun and two 7.62-mm machine guns, this was the Red Army's main battle tank in mid-1941. The new T-34 medium and KV heavy tanks had only started to trickle out to the frontier commands at the time of the invasion.

Retreating Soviet troops systematically destroyed rolling stock, watering stations, switching yards and infrastructure associated with their railroad network. As Stalin urged in a radio broadcast on 3 July 1941: leave not a 'single railway carriage, a single wagon, a single pound of grain for the enemy.'

Destroyed Soviet rolling stock. Although the Wehrmacht quickly assumed tactical and operational superiority over the Red Army in mid-1941, the primary problem lay in supplying the massive operation over increasing distances.

A column of German MAN E 3000 trucks with trailers. Some 3,000 of these vehicles were built for the Wehrmacht. Note the wrecked Soviet GAZ (*Gorkovsky Avtomobilny Zavod*) AAA truck in the foreground.

A mixed German column led by a Matford V8-F917-F997WS. In the foreground lies the wreck of a Soviet ZiS 5 truck.

Abandoned and stripped Soviet GAZ AA and MM trucks.

A column of German trucks flanked by shattered Soviet vehicles. In the foreground is a destroyed ZiS 5 truck, which together with the GAZ AA, formed the backbone of the Red Army truck park in June 1941.

The aftermath of battle: a tangled mass of wrecked Red Army GAZ AA and MM trucks.

Trümmer (wreckage). Scenes of destruction such as these attest to the enormous Soviet losses during the initial months of Barbarossa. The German truck is an Opel Blitz.

Destroyed Red Army transport. The smashed tanker is a Soviet ZiS 11 PMZ 2 or 3 fire fighting tanker.

A column of Ford V8-51 trucks on a road lined with Red Army wreckage. The tactical symbol 'N' on the vehicle's fender stands for *Nachschub* (supply unit).

Red Army soldiers lie dead beside their ZiS 5 truck. An estimated 8.7 million Soviet military personnel died in the war. In April 2015 a new law was passed by the Ukrainian Parliament to refer to the 'Great Patriotic War', as it was known in the USSR, as the Second World War.

The massive Stalino steelworks in ruins. In the wake of the German invasion, Nikita Khrushchev, future leader of the Soviet Union, implemented a massive programme to move machinery from Ukrainian factories and workshops by rail to the safety of the Urals and beyond, a 'second line of industrial defence'.

Greatcoated *Landser* alight from their Horch 108 Type 40 beside the wreckage of a Polikarpov I-16. Soviet pilots called the stubby fighter aircraft *Ishak* or 'Little Donkey'.

The Red Army launched an amphibious assault on the Kerch Peninsula between 26 and 30 December 1941 to relieve Soviet forces trapped at Sevastopol. The bridgehead survived for five months before General Erich von Manstein's German-led counteroffensive, Operation *Trappenjagd* (Bustard Hunt), destroyed the bridgehead and the three Soviet Armies supporting the landing in May 1942.

Chapter 8
Combat preparations

Watching for enemy activity from high ground. German defensive doctrine (*Verteidigung*, or *Abwehr*) aimed to halt an enemy attack, or to gain time for a more favourable situation in which to resume the offensive. Training emphasized the need for combat leaders to follow orders, but also encouraged flexibility, depending on the combat situation.

Dug-in positions above a river. Basic training taught the importance of utilizing terrain to optimal effect: 'Cover against armoured attack may require the use of natural barriers such as rivers, swamps and steep slopes.' As a general rule, in favourable terrain, a sector can be about twice as wide for defence as for attack.

A lull in the fighting. Note the MG34 machine gun and magazines. An officer from the 4th Panzer Division complained about German weaponry in the Soviet Union: the 'equipment, which proved efficient in the previous campaigns, was not robust enough for battle under the conditions prevailing in Russia. Russian equipment seemed to be more robust and less sensitive. Therefore, whoever got hold of a Russian tommy-gun kept it.'

Helmets off for this MG34 team while information is received from a field telephone. Each infantry squad possessed one of these automatic weapons.

Armed signal troops establishing telephone communication. Note the cable reels. Telephone lines of any distance were usually laid along roads and trails.

Keeping a close watch for the enemy from a subterranean observation post. The Army's *Truppenführung* (Unit Command) manual instructed that a 'well-constructed main battle area normally consists of a chain mutually supporting positions with obstacles, trenches, and individual firing positions. The defensive (*Abwehr*) is based primarily on firepower.'

The MG34 machine-gunner (No.1) operated the weapon in combat. He was also responsible for maintaining the weapon. To his left was his assistant (No.2), responsible for ensuring the supply of ammunition, correcting jams and changing barrels. Note the application of mud and an elastic band holding foliage on the *Stahlhelm* to aid camouflage.

Helmeted infantry, several carrying M1939 *Stielhandgranate* 43 stick grenades in their belts, pose for a group photograph during a pause in the fighting.

Although the German Panzerkampfwagen I and II (left and right respectively) were obsolete by mid-1941, both tanks formed a significant percentage of the German Panzerwaffe.

A casualty with a leg injury is brought in and dressed in the field. Front line units stressed that no more than two men were to bring back their wounded since their absence undermined available firepower.

The recoil operated, air cooled MG34 machine gun was a versatile weapon that operated on a number of different mounts and with different optical sights. Mounted on a tripod for anti-aircraft defence, this gun has a *Gurttrommel* 34 fifty-round basket magazine with two extra *Patronenkasten* 41 ammunition cans at the ready.

Chapter 9
The Dead and the Decorated

The grave of Colonel Ervin Claus, 8th Rumanian *Rosiori* (Cavalry) Division, killed during a Soviet air attack on the Kerch docks on 23 September 1942. At the time, his unit was preparing to cross the Kerch Strait from Crimea to the Taman Peninsula.

Obergefreiter Franz Baumgartner was killed on 23 June 1943 at Korostischew (Korostyshev). The oak leaf wreath, common on Wehrmacht badges and awards, symbolized strength, and the oak tree is renowned for its longevity. His candle-lit coffin is displayed at the *Ortskommandantur* (local commandant's) office before interment at the Hegewald military cemetery at Zhitomir (Zhytomyr) in northern Ukraine.

A large oak leaf wreath precedes the chaplain and pall-bearers. A German infantry division had two *Kriegspfarrer* (war chaplains), one Protestant and one Catholic. During a funeral service the Catholic chaplain would wear a vestment over his tunic.

Following a service by a Protestant chaplain, a volley of shots ring out while the coffin is lowered into the ground. The band in the background plays the national anthem.

An honour guard stands before the coffin of their fallen *Kamerad* at the Hegewald 'Heroes cemetery'. *Hegewald* (roughly translated as game reserve) was an experimental *Volksdeutsche* settlement established in Ukraine by Heinrich Himmler in 1942.

The temporary grave cross marks the resting place of Obergefreiter Franz Baumgartner. A regulation Wehrmacht grave cross would later mark his burial place.

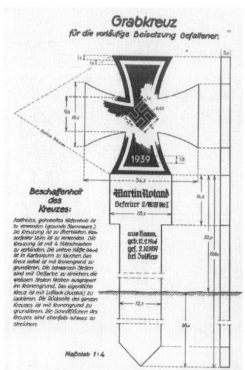

The final salute. *Obergefreiter* Karl Landvogt's coffin is lowered into the ground. Zhitomir cemetery was expanded after the war to accommodate graves exhumed from the surrounding area and today it holds the remains of 3,143 German soldiers killed in the bloodiest war in history.

A wounded soldier eulogizes and salutes a fallen comrade. Lamenting lost lives, a German combatant penned, 'The war has ripped my joy away from me. One can lose one's belief, one's love, one's reverence. Today I stand in external and internal struggle. Of my best friends the best have fallen… I don't know when I will again have peace.'

The temporary grave cross of *Obergefreiter* Karl Heinrich Landvogt, killed at B. Staroselyz b. Korostyshev on 1 August 1943.

The *Ostvolkmedaille*, or Medal for Gallantry and Merit for Members of the Eastern Peoples, was instituted on 14 July 1942 for *Ostvolk* rendering good service. Available in two classes, the decoration with crossed swords was awarded for gallantry. German troops serving with *Osttruppen* were eligible for this bravery award after November 1942 provided they had already received the Iron Cross. It was not until mid-1944 that Soviet volunteers were eligible to wear German awards.

Standing to attention while a comrade receives the Iron Cross. Regulations specified that 'the middle finger lies on the trouser seam, the thumb along the index finger on the inside of the hand. The head is held erect, the chin a little drawn back into the neck.'

Awarding the *Eisernes Kreuz 2. Klasse* (Iron Cross 2nd Class). King Frederick Wilhelm III of Prussia first introduced the bravery decoration in March 1813 while fighting the French under Napoleon. Hitler reinstituted the medal as a German decoration on 1 September 1939, bearing the swastika and suspended from a ribbon carrying the national colours: red, black and white.

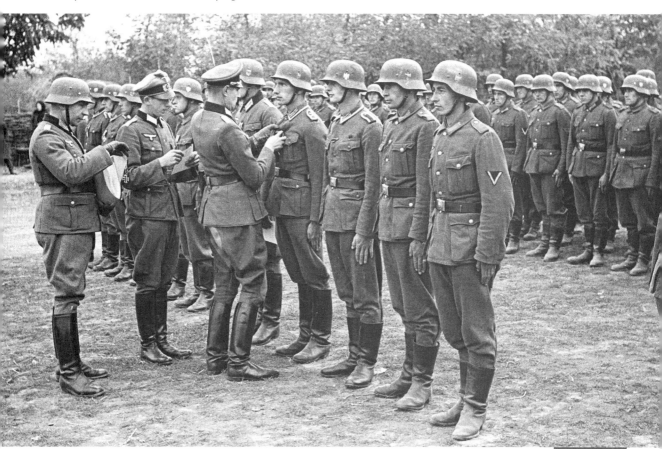

An officer addresses his assembled men. The *Stahlhelm* they wear was already obsolete by this time and work had commenced on a new design. Hitler, however, forbade the introduction of an alternative helmet since the existing one was symbolic of the 'Greater German Freedom Struggle'. The East German Army subsequently adopted the new model B/II helmet after the war.

The soldier on the right displays his newly awarded Iron Cross 2nd Class. The medal was only worn on the field uniform the day it was awarded; subsequently only the ribbon was worn. One of the iconic military awards of the twentieth century, some 300,000 1st Class and 2,300,000 2nd Class Iron Crosses were awarded during the war.

Decorating his men, this *Oberleutnant* wears his *Schirmmütze* without a cap spring to resemble the old-style officers' field or 'crusher' cap (*Feldmütze älterer* Art).

Landser look on as the identification tag of a moustached comrade is inspected.

Receiving a boxed decoration, the piped *Funkmeister* trade badge worn by this NCO identifies him as a radio specialist *Wachtmeister*.

Newly decorated NCOs pose with the War Merit Cross 2nd Class with Swords.

This *Oberfeldwebel* wears the *Kriegsverdienstkreuz II mit Schwertern* (War Merit Cross 2nd Class with Swords). The decoration was presented to military personnel for bravery not necessarily in the face of the enemy.

This *Unteroffizier* wears the predominately red ribbon of the *Ostmedaille* (Eastern Front Medal). The award was instituted on 26 May 1942 to recognize both combatants and noncombatants who saw service during the period 15 November 1941 to 26 April 1942. Inscribed *Winterschlacht im Osten* 1941/42 (Winter Battle in the East), the decoration was derided as the 'Order of the Frozen Flesh'.

Group portrait showing new recipients of the War Merit Cross 2nd Class with swords. A total of 6,134,950 of these medals were awarded to Germans and other nationalities who distinguished themselves in the service of the Third Reich.

Stern-faced soldiers celebrate Christmas. Hitler's campaign against the Soviet Union mirrored Napoleon's ill-fated nineteenth century campaign. As Clausewitz reflected, 'The Russia campaign of 1812 demonstrated in the first place that a country of such size could not be conquered (which might well have been foreseen), and in the second that the prospect of eventual success does always decrease in proportion to lost battles, captured capitals, and occupied provinces… On the contrary, the Russians showed us that one often attains one's greatest strength in the heart of one's own country, when the enemy's offensive power is exhausted, and the defensive can then switch with enormous energy to the offensive.'

Postscript

Walter Julius Grimm, grandson of the famous German scientific photographer Julius Grimm, was born in Offenburg, Germany, on 19 May 1911. After working for Lufthansa from 1935 to 1937 in aerial photography, he opened his own studio. Conscripted into the German Army in 1940, Grimm returned to photography after the war before retiring to Australia in 1984. He died on 22 December 2002.

Appendix 1

Chronology of the War in Ukraine

1939

23 August. Nazi Germany and the Soviet Union sign a Non-Aggression Pact in Moscow, dividing control over Eastern Europe.

1 September. Germany invades Poland. Two days later, Britain and France declare war on Germany.

17 September. The Soviet Union invades Poland from the east.

27 September. Warsaw falls to the Germans.

8 October. Poland is divided into two occupation zones with the western sector incorporated into the Third Reich.

1941

22 June. Hitler launches Operation Barbarossa, the invasion of the Soviet Union.

27 June. Hungary declares war on the Soviet Union.

30 June. Germans capture Lviv.

3 July. Stalin calls from a 'scorched earth' policy in a radio broadcast.

10–11 July. *Generalfeldmarschall* Fedor von Bock's Army Group Centre cross the Dniepr River. In the South, a Soviet counter-offensive fails. German tanks approach to within 10 miles of Kiev.

12 August. Hitler insists on the destruction of the Soviet South-West Front before resuming the advance in the Centre towards Moscow.

18–27 September 1941. Nearly two-thirds of the Red Army's strength on the outbreak of war has been eliminated.

19 September. German troops occupy Kiev. The occupation of the Ukrainian capital lasts 778 days.

26 September. 665,000 Soviet troops surrender in the Battle of Kiev, the largest army to surrender in military history.

20 October. Stalino falls to German and Italian forces.

23–24 October. *Generalfeldmarschall* Gerd von Rundstedt's Army Group South enters Kharkov.

30 November. Over 3.8 million Soviet soldiers surrender between 22 June and 30 November.

26–30 December. Red Army troops land on the Kerch Peninsula to relieve Sevastopol.

1942

January. A campaign starts to attract Ukrainian workers – *Ostarbeiter* (eastern workers) – to work in German war industries. Eventually some 2.3 million Ukrainians were deported, the majority forcibly.

15 May. German forces break through on the Crimean Front and occupy Kerch, forcing the Russians to evacuate the Kerch peninsula.

4 July. Sevastopol in Crimea falls after a 250-day siege.

13 July. Hitler issues orders simultaneous assaults against Stalingrad and the Caucasus.

9 August. Ukrainian soccer team FC '*Start*' defeats German team at Kiev and is executed.

21 August. German mountain troops reach the summit of Mount Elbrus in the Caucasus.

1943

2–3 January. Germans begin a withdrawal from the Caucasus.

31 January. German Sixth Army in Stalingrad surrenders.

16 February. Soviets re-take Kharkov.

15 March. Germans re-capture Kharkov.

5 July–23 August. German forces are defeated at the Battle of Kursk, on north-eastern border of Ukraine, in the greatest tank battle in history.

23 August. Soviet troops recapture Kharkov.

8 September. Italian surrender is announced.

25 October. Dnipropetrovsk captured by Soviet troops.

6 November. Kiev is retaken by Soviet troops.

1944

5 January. Beginning of Soviet campaign to retake Ukraine.

11 March. Soviet 2nd Ukrainian Front reaches the Bug River.

8 April. Soviet troops undertake offensive to liberate Crimea.

9 May. Soviet troops recapture Sevastopol.

12 May. Germans surrender in the Crimea.

14 October. German occupation of Ukrainian territory ends after 1,871 days.

1945

4–11 February. Yalta Conference in Crimea of the 'Big Three': Roosevelt, Churchill and Stalin.

30 April. Hitler commits suicide in his Berlin bunker.

8 May. V-E Day (Victory in Europe). Unconditional surrender of Germany after 2,076 days of war.

9 May. Prague captured by the Red Army: Soviet Victory Day.

Bibliography

Official Records—United States of America

Historical Division, Headquarters United States Army, Europe. *Signal Communications in the East: German Experience in Russia* by Albert Praun, *General der Nachrichtentruppen.* 1954.

Center of Military History, United States Army, Washington D.C. *Effects of Climate on Combat in European Russia.* February 1952.

Published Sources

Bartov, O. *Hitler's Army: Soldiers, Nazis, and War in the Third Reich.* Oxford, 1991.

Beevor, A. *The Second World War.* London 2012.

Berkhiff, K.C. *Harvest of Despair: Life and Death in Ukraine Under Nazi Rule.* London, 2004.

Bidermann, G.H. *In Deadly Combat: A German Soldier's Memoir on the Eastern Front.* Lawrence [Kansas], 2000.

Fritz, S.G. *Frontsoldaten: The German Soldier in World War II.* Lexington, 1995.

Glantz, D.M. *Operation Barbarossa: Hitler's Invasion of Russia 1941.* Stroud [Gloucestershire], 2012.

———. *Stumbling Colossus: The Red Army on the Eve of World War.* Lawrence [Kansas], 1998.

Hürter, J. *A German General on the Eastern Front: The Letters and Diaries of Gotthard Heinrici 1941-1942.* Barnsley, 2014.

Knappe, S. *Soldat: Reflections of a German Soldier, 1936-1949.* New York, 1992.

Metelmann, H. *Through Hell for Hitler.* London, 1990.

Neitzel, S. and H. Welzer. *Soldaten – On Fighting, Killing and Dying: The Secret WWII Transcripts of German POWS.* Melbourne, 2012.